100ᵗʰ Day of School

by Melissa Schiller

Content Consultants

Elizabeth Case DeSantis, M.A.
Julia A. Stark Elementary School, Stamford, Connecticut

Carrie A. Bell, MST Visual Arts – All Grades
Julia A. Stark Elementary School, Stamford, Connecticut

Reading Consultant

Jeanne M. Clidas, Ph.D.
Reading Specialist

Children's Press®
An Imprint of Scholastic Inc.
New York Toronto London Auckland Sydney
Mexico City New Delhi Hong Kong
Danbury, Connecticut

Library of Congress Cataloging-in-Publication Data
Schiller, Melissa.
    100th day of school / by Melissa Schiller.
      pages cm. — (Rookie read-about holidays)
    Includes index.
    ISBN 978-0-531-27200-8 (library binding) — ISBN 978-0-531-27350-0 (pbk.)
    1. Hundredth Day of School—Juvenile literature. I. Title. II. Title: Hundredth day of
school.
    LB3533.S35 2013
    372.18—dc23   2013014825

Produced by Spooky Cheetah Press

© 2014 by Scholastic Inc.

Printed in China 62

SCHOLASTIC, CHILDREN'S PRESS, ROOKIE READ-ABOUT®, and associated logos
are trademarks and/or registered trademarks of Scholastic Inc.

1 2 3 4 5 6 7 8 9 10 R 23 22 21 20 19 18 17 16 15 14

Photographs © 2014: Adam Chinitz: 28; AP Images/Joel Andrews, The Lufkin Daily
News: 27, 31 top; Louise Gardner: 7; Media Bakery: 16, 30 top right (Aluma Images),
12 (Katy McDonnell), 30 bottom, 31 bottom (Larry Washburn), 14, 30 top left (Ned
Frisk); Newscom/Zumapress: 20 (Brian Ramsay), 4 (Stan Carroll), 3 bottom, 24, 31
center bottom (The Bakersfield Californian); PhotoEdit/Bill Aron: 8, 11, 31 center top;
Shutterstock, Inc./kanusommer: 3 top; The Image Works: 23 (James Borchuck/St
Petersburg Times), 19 (Noah K. Murray/The Star-Ledger); Woodstone Elementary
School in North East ISD: cover.

Table of Contents

Hooray for 100!

The 100th Day of School is a very special day. We **celebrate** how much we have grown and learned. We are 100 days smarter than when we first started school! Hooray!

This girl made "100" glasses for her school celebration.

From the very first day of class, we started marking off days on the calendar. Soon we were more than **halfway** through the school year!

FAST FACT!

The 100th Day can be on different days in different schools. It depends on when school starts.

FEBRUARY

SUNDAY	MONDAY	TUESDAY	WEDNESDAY	THURSDAY	FRIDAY	SATURDAY
						1
2	3	4	5	6	7	8
9	10	11	12	13	14	15
16	17	18	19	20	21	22
23	24	25 **100th DAY**	26	27	28	

These kids are using charts to count to 100 by 1s.

Counting the Days in Different Ways

Our class did many fun math projects before the 100th Day. They all helped us learn about the number 100.

We each made a **collection** of 100 objects for a 100th Day Museum. Some children collected 100 pebbles. Others collected 100 beads. To make our collections, we counted by 1s.

This boy is sharing his collection of 100 stickers with the class.

We made a paper chain to hang around our classroom. We used different colors to make 100 links.

These girls are making stacks of 10 pennies. 100 cents add up to 1 dollar.

We counted 100 pennies and put them in a coin jar. We made 10 stacks of 10 pennies to make 100. That is counting by 10s.

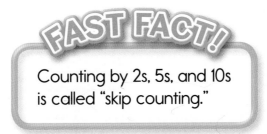

FAST FACT!

Counting by 2s, 5s, and 10s is called "skip counting."

16

We made a banner to hang in our classroom. We dipped our hands in paint to make handprints on it. There are 100 handprints on the banner.

Each set of handprints is made up of two hands. That is counting by 2s!

Celebrating 100 Days

We have reached the 100th Day of School. It is time to celebrate that we can count to 100! The class is having a party with snacks, crafts, and games.

These classmates are sharing a snack at their 100th Day celebration.

Shh! We try to stay quiet for 100 seconds. That feels like a long time!

This boy is trying not to giggle for 100 seconds.

We count how many jumping jacks we can do in 100 seconds.
Ready, set, jump!

The teachers are keeping track of how many jumping jacks the class does.

We wear 100th Day crowns. Each of us made our own crown and **decorated** it with 100 things.

This boy will add 100 stickers to his crown.

We released 100 balloons to celebrate the 100th Day of School. How will *you* celebrate?

These students watch as their 100 balloons take to the sky.

Make a 100th Day Necklace

What You'll Need

- Plastic string
- Scissors
- Tape
- 100 pony beads

Directions

1. With an adult's help, measure and cut enough string to make a necklace. Tie a knot at one end.

2. Place the knotted end in the middle of your table and place tape over the knot so that the string is secure. Then carefully begin stringing.

3. Add the beads, one at a time, to the string. Make a pattern or string random beads—whichever you like best!

4. When you have added the 100 beads, tie a knot on the opposite end of the string. Then tie the two ends of the string together and wear your 100th Day necklace.

Show What You Know!

Let's Skip Count!

- Which of these photos shows counting by 2s?
- Which shows counting by 10s?
- How do you know?

Let's Measure!

- Make a paper clip chain by linking 100 paper clips together.
- Use your chain like a ruler to measure. What is longer than your chain? What is shorter?

What Did You Learn?

On your 100th Day, make a list of three things you learned in the first 100 days of school.

Glossary

celebrate (SEL-uh-brate): to do something fun on a special occasion

collection (kuh-LEK-shuhn): a group of similar objects

decorated (DEK-uh-rate-ed): added things to make something prettier

halfway (haf-way) half the distance from one point to another

Index

Facts for Now

Visit this Scholastic Web site for more information
on the 100th Day of School:
www.factsfornow.scholastic.com
Enter the keywords **100th Day**

About the Author

Melissa Schiller taught second grade for five years. Now she tutors
students in reading and writing in her home in New York City. Melissa
and her husband are the proud parents of two teenage boys and
Ginger, their darling wheaten terrier.